CreatingCareerConnections

CreatingCareerConnections

A Pre-College to Career Enrichment Guide

Second Edition

Lesia M. Banks, Ed.D., MBA

C³ CreatingCareerConnections
A Pre-College to Career Enrichment Guide
All Rights Reserved.
Copyright © 2017 Lesia M. Banks, ED.D., MBA
2nd Edition

This book may not be reproduced, transmitted, or stored in whole by any means, including graphic, electronic, or mechanical without the express written consent of the publisher.

Aisel Alliance Publishing Group

ISBN: 978-0-692-96342-5

Cover Photo © 2017 Lesia M. Banks, ED.D., MBA. All rights reserved – used with permission.

Cover Design: SPJ Graphic Designs, Inc.: SPJGraphicDesigns@gmail.com.

Author Photograph:
StephAnn Photography – www.facebook.com/StephAnnPhotography.
LaTasha Wilson Averett – www.facebook.com/LaTasha-Wilson-Averett.

PRINTED IN THE UNITED STATES OF AMERICA

"In youth we learn; in age we understand."

-Marie von Ebner-Eshenbach

Dedicated to every person who has
ever been told, "You can't……"

FOREWORD

When this beautiful child, Lesia Banks, came into the world, little did the small town community of Danville, Virginia know that a sparkling jewel had come forth; one whose heart was embossed with stewardship, compassion, dedication, and love for service to mankind that emulated the highest calling of Love, Agape. Dr. Banks' entire life has been one of preparation that would ready her to empty that heart of stewardship; emptying hers to fill others whenever and wherever the void. The preparation was not always easy; it never is when your focus is for others as hers has been. A well spent journey is usually filled with climbing mountains and forging valleys but always dreaming of beautiful fields of flowers to pick and give to others and now she walks in those flanders fields picking and giving, picking and giving and yes, between the pages of this book she is still giving; direction, examples, illustrations and word pictures that if followed others will receive and be filled as she intended.

Mrs. Carrie Peeler Ashe
Retired, Administrator of Education
Danville Public School System

PREFACE

The first person to ever ask me what I wanted to be when I grew up was my high school guidance counselor. I happily and proudly told her that I wanted to be a lawyer. She continued our conversation by asking me which classes I liked. She also asked about the ones I disliked. I told her that I loved History and Reading, but I did not like Math. I still vividly remember the declaration she made: "Since you do not like math, you cannot be a lawyer. You should register for a secretarial program instead." I was crushed. I thought my dreams were, too. I wanted so badly to study criminal law and to become a criminal defense attorney. I could envision myself standing before a judge, jury, and prosecutor. I could imagine crowds of spectators listening intently from the galley. I could hear myself defending and representing my client. Sadly, my guidance counselor, a person who was charged to give me encouragement and direction, did little more than quash my dreams. Believing her to be an expert, I had no idea if my dream could be resurrected.

I was raised by blue collar, hard-working parents who, unfortunately, didn't have the tools necessary to give me the needed guidance to achieve academic success beyond high school. Perplexed and daunted by my guidance counselor's words, I enrolled in the Liberal Arts program at Danville Community College. At the beginning of the second quarter I registered for a criminal law class and I fell in love with the study of law. My dream hadn't died, it has only been dazed. The revered and iconic Criminal Law professor, Gordon Brooks Powell, taught me with diligence and passion "the thundering rule of law." Under his tutelage, a seed was sown that would one day result in blossoming academic success. I earned not only an Associate's degree, but a Bachelor's, Master's, and eventually a terminal degree—my doctorate of Education.

As I was researching information for this book, I repeatedly said to myself, "I wish I would have known this!" "I wish I would have known that!" "Where was this information as I was trying to figure out how to maneuver through high school, college, and a career?" I have such a passion for people and for learning. If I could help it, not another student would allow one person's declaration or opinion to destroy their dreams.

This book is expressly designed to assist individuals in setting and accomplishing their career goals. It is intended to serve as a reference guide for those who are entering the workforce in entry level positions. I love researching and used my skills to gather as much information as possible. It's a one stop shop for college bound individuals, as young as middle school aged students, that will provide the reader with a checklists and action plans to consult and follow. It provides steps on how to succeed in college. It also provides information on resumes and cover letters, and advice for surviving an interview. It gives tips on how to maintain a position and thrive in it. It also provides numerous tips on successful networking.

The book doesn't merely contain my opinions and insights. It includes information from the foremost authorities on education and careers, including the United States Department of Education, the United States Department of Labor and nationally-known career development experts.

The renowned 19th century poet, Ralph Waldo Emerson said, "Sow a thought and you reap an action; sow an act and you reap a habit; sow a habit and you reap a character; sow a character and you reap a destiny."

In this book I have attempted to sow the thoughts, actions, habits, and character traits that are paramount to scholarly and career success. By reading this book you will reap information and insight, and understand the actions, habits, and character traits that pave the road to a career destiny laden with success.

You *can* excel. You *can* be a lawyer, doctor, chef, CEO, teacher, engineer, or an entrepreneur. You *can* be whatever your mind can imagine. CREATING an environment that breeds academic and CAREER success is ultimately your responsibility. CONNECTIONS are resources. Don't neglect to utilize them.

ACKNOWLEDGMENT

One of my favorite songs is The Crabb Family's "Through the Fire". The song articulates the sentiments of my heart and echoes my love for Christ and appreciation for his place in my life. "He never promised that the cross would not get heavy, and the hill would not be hard to climb. He never offered victories without fighting, but He said help would always come in time. Just remember when you're standing in the valley of decision and the adversary says, "Give in!" just hold on--our Lord will show up, and yes, take you through the fire again."

It is with a heart of thankfulness and humbleness that I express my sincerest gratitude to my Lord and Savior Jesus Christ for giving me the ability and desire to write this book. A desire to help others is a wonderful sign of his spirit revealed in me.

I extend sincere gratitude to Dexter M. Montgomery, a co-worker, who through a simple networking session unknowingly sowed the seed for this book.

I am eternally grateful for Averett University president, Dr. Tiffany Franks, for her support, encouragement, timely advice, and assistance and for excitedly launching this book's initial release during my alma mater's 2014 Homecoming festivities.

I would also like to thank my immediate family for their positive impact in my life. To my grandmother, Edith Banks Wimbish; my mother, Susie Banks Grasty; my late father, Robert Wayne Grasty; and my siblings, Margaret, Sharon, Debra, and Robert, thank you.

Last, but certainly not least, I would like to especially thank my soul mate, partner for life, and greatest supporter, the brilliant Dr. Alvin Brown, whose own story of success and accomplishment (three earned degrees--Bachelor of Science in Chemistry, Master of Science in Analytical Chemistry and Doctor of Dental Medicine) is a lesson in the value of education, and my niece, now eight year-old Sydney Marie Hall, who will one day be able to use this book as a resource for her own educational and career advancement.

CONTENTS

SECTION I: CREATING

CREATING 23
    Junior High or Middle School 26
    Every Year in High School 28
    9th Grade 30
    10th Grade 32
    11th Grade 34
    Summer-- Before 12th Grade 37
    12th Grade 39
    MY NEXT MOVE: Fact Sheet 45
    What is the My Next Move electronic tool? 45
    10 Tips for Freshman Success 52
    TEN STEPS TO COLLEGE SUCCESS 55
    Notes 62

SECTION II: CAREER

CAREER 67
    CDDQ-Career Decision-making Difficulties Questionnaire. 70
    CCDD-Coping with Career Decision-making Difficulties
    Questionnaire 70
    EPCD-Emotional and Personality related Career Decision
    Difficulties 71
    CDMP-Career Decision Making Profile (style) 71

- PC-Preference Crystallization 71
- PIC-Pre-screening, In-depth Exploration, Choice 72
- CHOICE 72
- SUSIE Q. EXAMPLE 74
- Professional Summary 74
- Core Qualifications 74
- Experience 74
- Education 75
- Professional Affiliations 75
- COVER LETTERS 79
  - DO YOUR RESEARCH FIRST 79
  - OPEN STRONG 80
  - EMPHASIZE YOUR PERSONAL VALUE 81
  - CONVEY ENTHUSIASM 81
  - BE BRIEF 82
  - WHEN YOU CAN'T SUBMIT A COVER LETTER 83
- INTERVIEWS 85
  - RESEARCH 87
  - PRACTICE, PRACTICE, PRACTICE 88
  - KNOW THE LOGISTICS 88
  - BE PROMPT AND PROFESSIONAL 88
  - DRESS FOR SUCCESS 89
  - BE ORGANIZED 90
  - KNOW YOURSELF 90
  - BE HONEST 91
  - BE POSITIVE 91
  - DISPLAY INTEREST 91
  - TALK MONEY LATER 92
  - POST-INTERVIEW NOTES 92
  - FOLLOW UP 92

QUESTIONS, QUESTIONS, QUESTIONS! 94
"BASIC INTERVIEW" QUESTIONS 95
"BEHAVIORAL INTERVIEW" QUESTIONS 96
"SALARY" QUESTIONS 98
"CAREER DEVELOPMENT" QUESTIONS 99
"GETTING STARTED" QUESTIONS 100
"MORE ABOUT YOU" QUESTIONS 101
"BRAINTEASER" QUESTIONS 104
SUCCESS AT WORK 118
MAINTAINANCE 118
TO THRIVE 120
Notes 121

SECTION III: CONNECTIONS

CONNECTIONS 125
   How Do People Find Jobs? 127
   Professional Networking 128
   Getting Ahead: Tips For Social Networking 131
   Don't expect social networking
      to be a magic career wand 131
   Do present a consistent, professional
      profile in social networking bios 131
   Use Alltop.com to find other niche bloggers. 132
   Use WeFollow.com or Listorious.com to find Twitter
      users who share professional interests. 132
   Use online platforms to pass along useful
      professional advice and information. 133
   Informational Interviews: What They Are, and Why
      They Are Pertinent to Career Success 134
   Networking for Business Building 136

NETWORKING FOR INTROVERTS 140
NETWORKING FOR EXTROVERTS 146
   Notes 151
REFERENCES 153

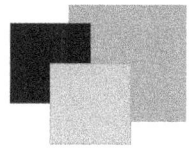

SECTION I: CREATING

CREATING

"I've missed more than 9000 shots in my career. I've lost almost 300 games. Twenty-six times, I've been trusted to take the game winning shot, and missed. I've failed over and over and over again in my life. And that is why I succeed."

-Michael Jordan

The burden is on you to CREATE the opportunity and environment for success.

A college education is a keystone to career success. Before you can succeed in college, however, you must first understand the college admission process! You may have already asked yourself these questions: Will I be accepted by the college(s) of my choice? Will I succeed in college? Will I graduate with my desired degree?

You must understand that the likelihood of whether you will succeed in college is not determined when you are finally in college. It starts as early as middle school. You must know what classes to take that will allow you the greatest opportunity to be

SECTION I: CREATING

accepted to your college(s) of choice. You must also realize that grades and test scores are very important, even those earned as early as the 8th and 9th grade. If you plan to wait until you are a high school senior to be diligent about your grades, you will have waited too late!

Obtaining a college degree does more than just educate you in the curriculum you've chosen, it provides access to a world of cultural and networking opportunities that are sure to benefit you throughout the entire span of your professional career.

Although the main focus of this book is the transition from college to career; these next few pages are dedicated to preparing for college.

C3 Creating Career Connections

The United States Department of Education developed a series of check-lists that highlight what you need to do and subjects you need to explore as early as Junior High and Middle School to better your chances of college acceptance. These check-lists are valuable, and if followed, can help you prepare for your future!

The entire "To Do" list, which also includes a "To Do" list for parents, can be found at https://studentaid.ed.gov/sites/default/files/college-prep-checklist.pdf. I suggest that you save this site among your on-line favorites.

SECTION I: CREATING

WHEN TO DO IT:

Junior High or Middle School

No. You are neither too young nor too busy. Time will pass quickly. Use your time wisely. In choosing electives, be wise. Don't assume that certain grades or classes don't matter. Take each course seriously. Take advantage of mentoring and counseling services. This is also the time to remember that recommendations from teachers matter greatly. Mind your manners, attitude and work habits. Even if you have no idea what you want to be, remember the upper hand that a college education can give you when you enter the world of work.

WHAT TO DO:

- ☐ Think about college as an important part of your future. Discuss your thoughts and ideas with your family, schoolmates, teachers, counselors and coaches.
- ☐ Start saving for college if you haven't already.
- ☐ Select challenging and interesting classes to prepare for high school.

C3 CreatingCareerConnections

- ☐ Ask your parent or guardian to help you research which high schools or special programs align most with your interests and provide maximum benefit.
- ☐ Study habits matter. Develop useful ones.
- ☐ Do your best in school and on standardized tests. If you are having difficulty, get discouraged or give up—don't be afraid to seek help from a teacher, tutor, or mentor.
- ☐ Become involved in school or community-based activities that allow you to explore your interests and learn new skills, information and ideas.
- ☐ Speak with adults, such as your teacher, school counselor, librarian, relatives, or family friends who you think have interesting jobs. Ask them, "What do you like about your job?" and "What education or skills did you need in order to obtain your job?"

EXPLORE:

- ☐ Find out why you should prepare for college now. Information can be found at StudentAid.gov/prepare.
- ☐ Explore the workbook, "My Future, My Way: First Steps toward College". It is tailored to middle and junior high school students. StudentAid.gov/resources#my-future.

SECTION I: CREATING

WHEN TO DO IT:

Every Year in High School

Have fun, make friends, sleep, but remember graduation day is coming. You want to be in that line. Graduating with honors is not for a select few. You can do it.

WHAT TO DO:

- ☐ Work with your parents to estimate how much financial aid is available to you using FAFSA4caster at www.fafsa4caster.ed.gov, and continue to save for college.

- ☐ Take challenging classes in core academic subjects. Most colleges require four years of English, at least three years of Social Studies (History, Civics, Geography, Economics, etc.), three years of Mathematics, and three years of Science. Many colleges require two years of a foreign language. Computer Science, The Fine Arts, and Physical Education should be priorities as well.

- ☐ Stay involved in school or community-based activities that are of interest to you or allow you to explore career

C3 Creating Career Connections

interests. Consider working or volunteering. Remember, quality not quantity counts most.

- ☐ Continue to keep in touch with your school counselor and mentors after high school. Your counselor can not only answer questions about what classes to take in high school, and how to sign up for scheduled standardized tests, but may have vast knowledge about internships and scholarships.

EXPLORE:

- ☐ Check out KnowHow2Go: The Four Steps to College, which suggests some steps you can take as you start exploring education beyond high school. The online version of the brochure is at www.knowhow2go.org.
- ☐ Get answers to common questions about college by watching U.S. Department of Education videos on the "Prepare for College" playlist at www.YouTube.com/FederalStudentAid.
- ☐ Learn about managing your money from "Start Smart: Money Management for Teens" at www.fdic.gov /consumers /consumer /news /cnsum06 /sum_06_color.pdf.

SECTION I: CREATING

WHEN TO DO IT:

9th Grade

Remember, there's no time like the present. There's no such thing as too early to think about your future.

WHAT TO DO:

- ☐ Talk to your guidance counselor or teachers about Advanced Placement courses. Find out what courses are available, whether you are eligible, and how to enroll in them.

- ☐ Use the career search tool at StudentAid.gov/careersearch to research your career options.

- ☐ Make a list of your awards, honors, paid and volunteer work, and extracurricular activities. Consider participating in academic enrichment programs, summer workshops, and camps with specialty focuses such as Music, Art, and Science.

C3 CreatingCareerConnections

EXPLORE:

- ☐ Visit StudentAid.gov/why college, for great reasons to consider college.
- ☐ Find ways to get help preparing for college at StudentAid.gov /prepare-for-college/help.

SECTION I: CREATING

WHEN TO DO IT

10th Grade

Don't become lax. Stay on top of your grades, assignments, activities, and projects.

WHAT TO DO

- ☐ Meet with your school counselor or mentor to discuss colleges and their requirements.
- ☐ Take a *practice* Preliminary SAT/National Merit Scholarship Qualifying Test (PSAT/NMSQT®), or PSAT™ 10, or the PreACT™.
- ☐ Plan to use your summer wisely: Work, volunteer, or take a summer course (away or at a local college).
- ☐ Go to career information events.
- ☐ Research majors that might be a good fit with your interests and goals based on your results from the career search at StudentAid.gov/careersearch.

C3 CreatingCareerConnections

EXPLORE:

- ☐ Learn the differences between grants, loans, work-study, and scholarships at StudentAid.gov/types.
- ☐ Think about starting to research different colleges. Play around with the College Scorecard tool at collegescorecard.ed.gov to explore schools based on size, location, programs, and more.

SECTION I: CREATING

WHEN TO DO IT:

11th Grade

Stay focused. Soon you will be a senior!

WHAT TO DO:

All year:

- ☐ Explore various careers. The Occupational Outlook Handbook will also inform you about earning potential. www.bls.gov/oco.
- ☐ Learn about choosing a college (and find a link to the U.S. Department of Education's free college search tool) at StudentAid.gov /prepare-for-college /choosing-schools.
- ☐ Plan to attend college fairs and college-preparation presentations given by college representatives.

Fall:

- ☐ Take the PSAT/NMSQT.* It must be taken in 11th grade in order for students to qualify for scholarships

C3 CreatingCareerConnections

and programs associated with the National Merit Scholarship Program.

Spring:

- ☐ Register for and take exams for college admission.* The tests that many colleges require are the SAT, the SAT Subject Tests, and the ACT. Check with the colleges you are interested in to see what tests they require.
- ☐ Use the free scholarship search tool at studentaid.gov/scholarships to find scholarships for which you might want to apply. Some deadlines fall as early as the summer between 11th and 12th grades, so prepare now to submit applications soon.

EXPLORE:

- ☐ Visit www.YouTube.com/FederalStudentAid and go to the "Types of Aid" playlist to see how the government can help you pay for college.
- ☐ Learn how to avoid scholarship scams and identity theft at StudentAid.gov/scams.

SECTION I: CREATING

*REMEMBER: Register for all tests in advance, and be sure to give yourself time to prepare mentally and physically! If you have difficulty paying a registration fee, see your school counselor about obtaining a fee waiver.

WHEN TO DO IT:

Summer-- Before 12th Grade

Don't lose focus now! You're almost there. You are approaching the finish line and graduation day is just over the horizon, but first there will be a litany of once in a lifetime events: Homecoming, Prom, Senior Day, and of course written or oral examination days and project/assignment due dates--which are *very* important.

WHAT TO DO:

- ☐ Create a username and password called an FSA ID that you'll use to confirm your identity when accessing your government financial aid information and electronically signing your federal student aid documents. You and your parent will each need your own unique FSA ID. Learn about the FSA ID, and create yours, at StudentAid.gov/fsaid. Note: You must create your own FSA ID; if your parent creates it for you, that'll cause confusion later and will slow down the financial aid application process.

SECTION I: CREATING

- ☐ Narrow down the list of colleges you are considering attending. If you can, visit the schools that interest you.

- ☐ Contact colleges and request information, and admissions applications. Ask about financial aid, admission requirements, and deadlines.

- ☐ Decide whether you are going to apply using a particular college's early decision or early action program. Be sure to learn about the program deadlines and requirements.

- ☐ Apply for scholarships. Your goal is to minimize the amount of loan funds you borrow so you have less to pay back later.

EXPLORE:

- ☐ Find out what government financial aid you can apply for, and how, in *Federal Student Aid at a Glance* at StudentAid.gov/glance.

- ☐ Watch the "Overview of the Financial Aid Process" video at www.YouTube.com/FederalStudentAid to learn about getting student aid from the government.

- ☐ Be careful when searching for scholarships: Read "Don't Get Scammed on Your Way to College!" at StudentAid.gov/resources#consumer-protection to learn how to avoid getting cheated out of money.

WHEN TO DO IT:

12th Grade

WOW! In 10 months Graduation Day will be a reality! After years and years of preparation you can bask in your accomplishments, but don't start to slack off or rest on your laurels (or pillows). Remember that second semester grades DO count.

WHAT TO DO:

All year:

- ☐ Work hard all the way to graduation—second-semester grades can affect scholarship eligibility.
- ☐ Stay involved in after-school activities, and seek leadership roles if possible.

Fall:

- ☐ As soon as possible after its October 1 release, complete and submit your Free Application for Federal Student Aid (FAFSA®) at FAFSA.gov, along with any other financial aid applications your school(s) of choice

SECTION I: CREATING

may require. You should submit your FAFSA by the earliest financial aid deadline of the schools to which you are applying, usually by early February.

- [ ] After you submit the FAFSA, you should receive your *Student Aid Report* within three days to three weeks. This document lists your answers to the questions on your FAFSA and gives you some basic information about your aid eligibility. Quickly make any necessary corrections and submit them to the FAFSA processor.
- [ ] If you haven't done so already, register for and take such exams as the SAT, SAT Subject Tests, or ACT for college admission.* Check with the colleges you are interested in to see what tests they require.
- [ ] Apply to colleges you have chosen. Prepare your applications carefully. Follow the instructions, and PAY CLOSE ATTENTION TO DEADLINES!
- [ ] Ask your counselors and teachers to submit required documents (e.g., transcripts, letters of recommendation) to the colleges to which you have applied long before deadlines are looming.
- [ ] Complete any last scholarship applications.

*REMEMBER: Register for all tests in advance and be sure to give yourself time to prepare appropriately! If you have difficulty paying a registration fee, see your school counselor.

C3 CreatingCareerConnections

Spring:

- ☐ Take a trip! Visit the colleges and universities to which you have been invited to matriculate.

- ☐ Review your college acceptances and compare the colleges' financial aid offers. Use the "Compare Financial Aid Offers" tool at www.consumerfinance.gov/paying-for-college to analyze aid offers side by side.

- ☐ Contact a school's financial aid office if you have questions about the aid that school has offered you. In fact, getting to know your financial aid staff early is a good idea no matter what—they can tell you about deadlines, other aid for which you might wish to apply, and important paperwork you might need to submit.

- ☐ Are you collecting acceptance letters? Don't just celebrate. *Notify* the school of your intent, and remit any required financial deposit. Many schools require notification and deposit by May 1.

SECTION I: CREATING

EXPLORE:

- ☐ Refer to StudentAid.gov/fafsa to learn about the FAFSA process.
- ☐ Understand the FAFSA better by watching the videos in the "FAFSA: Apply for Aid" playlist at www.YouTube.com /FederalStudentAid.
- ☐ Follow or like the office of Federal Student Aid at www.Twitter.com /FAFSA and www.Facebook.com / FederalStudentAid to get regular financial aid tips.
- ☐ Make informed decisions about student loans; find important information at the "Federal Versus Private Loans pages at studentaid.gov/federal-vs-private.

C3 CreatingCareerConnections

NOTES:

SECTION I: CREATING

MyNextMove.org is a Career Search Tool hosted by the United States Department of Labor. Utilizing this tool can help you better identify a career choice and will provide information on what education is needed for success in that career. Consequently, it will help you identify an appropriate college major.

C3 CreatingCareerConnections

MY NEXT MOVE: Fact Sheet

What is the My Next Move electronic tool?

- My Next Move is an easy-to-use electronic tool that enables users to explore occupations and find related information, including job openings, job outlook information, salaries, apprenticeships, and other related education and training programs.

- My Next Move uses information developed as part of the Occupational Information Network (O*NET) system. Sponsored by the U.S. Department of Labor, Employment and Training Administration, O*NET is a comprehensive career information resource which collects data including the knowledge, skills, and abilities required by more than 900 occupations in the U.S. economy. (See Section II: Career (of this book), for detailed information on O*NET).

- Through this new electronic tool, users can search for careers using key words that align with industries

SECTION I: CREATING

or work-related interests. Occupations in the green economy can also be identified.

- The tool is written at a reading level that makes it accessible to everyone and is great for those who may be unfamiliar with computers and Internet sites.

- The tool includes a new on-line, streamlined interest assessment with 60 questions about what an individual likes to do. Based on an individual's interests and responses, the information gathered will be used to suggest potentially suitable occupations and careers.

Who Can Use the My Next Move electronic tool?

- My Next Move can be used by almost everyone and is available free, on-line at www.mynextmove.org. It was especially designed for students, youth, and others new to the workforce.

- The tool also can be accessed nationwide at One-Stop Career Centers, educational institutions, private industry, and state employment service.

C3 CreatingCareerConnections

What is O*NET?

- The O*NET system is the only comprehensive source of information on the knowledge, skills, abilities, work tasks, tools, technology, and other important requirements needed to perform work for occupations covering the entire U.S. economy.

- Data is collected on an ongoing basis from a national, representative sample of incumbent workers, as well as subject matter experts and job analysts. To date, over 40,000 businesses and 150,000 workers have participated in the O*NET data collection efforts.

- The Employment and Training Administration has a cooperative grant agreement with the North Carolina Employment Security Commission to conduct O*NET data collection and develop and maintain the O*NET Web sites and career exploration tools.

What Information Can You Obtain from My Next Move?

- Examples of alternative occupations/job titles used for the area of expertise

SECTION I: CREATING

- Concise descriptions of what people in specific occupations actually do

- The information, skills, and abilities which are most important for performing the occupation

- The key personality attributes necessary to perform the job

- Average national pay for the occupation, as well as a link to local salary information

- Direct links to job openings through www.mySkillsmyFuture.org and links to state and national job banks

- A symbol showing whether the occupation is classified as a "green" job

Web address: www.mynextmove.org
DOL Landing page: http://mynextmove.dol.gov
News Release: http://www.dol.gov/opa/media/press/eta/eta20101786.htm

C3 Creating Career Connections

Now that you have researched different careers, applied and have been accepted into college you are a giant step closer to achieving your career goals!

SECTION I: CREATING

Kasey Klepfer, an Archer Graduate Fellow at the University of Texas at Austin, and Jim Hull, Senior Policy Analyst, The Center for Public Education, National School Boards Association, presented research titled, "Setting up Students to Succeed". In their research they found that approximately two-thirds of the future jobs in the United States will require some sort of post-secondary education. Job reports show that by 2018, there will be 47 million jobs created by new industries. Simultaneously, there will be a retiring workforce (Carnevale, Smith and Strohl 2010). Of these jobs, 33 percent will require at least a bachelor's degree and 30 percent will require an associate's degree or some college training (Carnevale, Smith and Strohl 2010).

The report also found that the demand for workers with a college education is growing faster than the supply of graduates. By 2018, we will have produced 3 million fewer college graduates than the labor market demands (Carnevale, Smith and Strohl 2010). The report also indicates that President Obama set a national goal to produce 8 million more graduates by 2020 in order to make the United States the world leader in higher education. (You can retrieve the entire 22 page report of study at www.centerforpubliceducation.org.)

The study concluded that one effective way to get us on the path to reaching this goal is to prevent the students who enter college from leaving before they earn their credentials.

C3 CreatingCareerConnections

What do you need to do to CREATE an environment for success in college? Turn the page and you will find 10 Tips for Freshman Success and 10 More Tips for overall College Success!!!

SECTION I: CREATING

The 10 Tips for Freshman Success listed below were created by education expert, Tanya Knight. She is the author of "Who Says You Can't Go to College" and is known as "America's Education Coach." Her organization (www.TanyaKnight.com) aids parents and students of all ages through the path to higher education. These tips as well as additional information can be found at: http://www.firstgenerationstudent.com/blog/10-steps-freshmen-need-to-know-to-be-successful-in-college/.

10 Tips for Freshman Success

- **Communicate With Professors/ Instructors**: Contact each of your professors and ask for tips and advice specific to their classes. Often, instructors assume that all students "know" how things are. Asking direct questions will help you to fully understand the expectations and requirements set forth by each instructor.

- **Join Study Groups:** Making friends is good, but making valuable connections is, too. Join study groups. Don't be too proud to ask for and accept help. Seek others who have more knowledge or expertise, share information, listen, observe, adapt and change where appropriate.

C3 Creating Career Connections

- **Involve Yourself in Activities on Campus or Online**: The more time you spend on campus, the easier your transition will be, and the more you will meet others who share your interests. If you are in an online program, the discussion boards and chat rooms can be helpful. Seek out and participate in as many curricular and extra-curricular activities as possible, both on and off campus.

- **Count Oneself as Part of the Group**: Do not shy away from speaking in class, or in a group. Your voice really matters. The question you ask may help others. Force yourself to join in, and very soon you won't feel so isolated.

- **Keep Your Family Informed**: Just as you are anxious, your family is, too. They—especially your parents—want the best for you and they should be kept abreast of your progress and decisions. Communicate with your family and keep them in the loop, so that they can continue to support and motivate you to complete your program.

- **Seek Employment Opportunities**: Money will likely be one of your more pressing challenges. It is always good to seek out employment opportunities so that you

SECTION I: CREATING

can balance your academic life and expenses and reduce pressure and stress.

- **Ask Questions**: It is okay to not know everything. Ask questions when you are in doubt! It is much better to ask once and get the right answer than to keep wondering if you have the right information.

- **Believe That Attending College is a** Major **Achievement**: You worked hard, followed the rules, and didn't quit! You should be proud and feel happy about your accomplishments! Don't shrink!

- **Find and Enroll in Remedial Classes**: It is important that you feel really confident and prepared to take on college courses. Most students, who obtained above average grades in high school, find that they lag behind in certain subjects at college. Do not let this discourage you. Seek remedial classes and catch up.

- **Become a Part of the Alumni and Student Network**: Networking is a powerful way to establish working relationships, gain important information, build your confidence, learn of opportunities, and develop a sense of belonging. Align yourself with alumni and students who share your curricular and extra-curricular interests. A community of positive, encouraging peers is valuable while in college.

TEN STEPS TO COLLEGE SUCCESS

The City College of San Francisco developed 10 Steps to College Success. The steps are listed below and can also be found at www.ccsf.edu.

Step 1 – **Attend Every Class**
- Although "cutting" class may be tempting, *don't* do it if you can help it. Absences should be reserved for real emergencies that you cannot avoid. When you miss class, you miss lectures, notes, explanations of assignments, class discussions, and sometimes quizzes and in-class assignments. Getting copies of a classmate's notes won't always help.

Step 2 – **Get Organized**
- Get a weekly planner and use it religiously.

SECTION I: CREATING

- Create and maintain a tidy and organized study space, complete with everything that you need when you're working: paper, pens, pencils, stapler, etc.

- Use a separate 3-ring binder for each class you're taking.

- Back-up all of your computer files on drives, disks, flash drives, or by emailing them to your personal account.

- Keep all papers, quizzes and tests that you get back from your teachers at least until the final grades are submitted. If it's a course related to your major, you may want to keep them until you graduate.

- Get your classmates contact information so you can call or email them for study help, or to ask a question.

Step 3 – **Manage Your Time**

- Procrastination and you do not mix. Know when your assignments are due. Don't procrastinate. Break large tasks down into smaller, manageable ones.

- Set definite boundaries and limits. Spreading yourself too thin will only make you more tired and less able to function at your highest level.

- Time management and reservation of resources require efficiency. Limit yourself to a reasonable amount of TV and socializing time. Use those activities as rewards for getting your work done. Always look for ways to streamline or combine tasks (i.e., study while you're waiting for the bus, doing laundry, riding a stationary bicycle.)

Step 4 – **Use the Classroom to Succeed**
- Early birds are neither nerdy nor filled with anxiety. No one has *ever* had to apologize or make an excuse for being on time. Sit in the front row whenever you can.
- Ask questions and participate every chance you get.
- Talk with your instructors. Meet them during their posted office hours. Make sure they know your name and that you're committed to learning.
- Learn how to adapt to the teaching styles and requirements of your instructors.
- Join study groups and discussion groups based on the class subject, and be a good group member.

Step 5 – **Take Concise Notes**
- Find a note taking system that works for you, such as Cornell, mind maps, or outlines.
- Listen actively. Focus on the speaker, think, and try to understand the topic being presented.

SECTION I: CREATING

- Learn to recognize the important information by paying attention to verbal and nonverbal clues your instructor gives. If he or she raises their voice, speaks more slowly, writes something down on the board, or repeats it, it's probably important. If the information being discussed also appears in the textbook, it's probably important. Look for the signs.
- Make sure your notes are legible and have plenty of white space.
- Review your notes within 24 hours of taking them.

Step 6 – **Actively Read Your Textbook**
- Beds are for sleeping. Reading posture and location may be the difference between absorbing the information you need and missing it altogether. Sit up straight with your book on a bookstand, or held in front of you instead. Active reading happens more when a body is more active than at rest.

Step 7 – **Study Smart**
- Find a good place to study: the library, a quiet area in your house, wherever you can work best. It should be comfortable, well lit, fully stocked, and free of distractions.

- Remember that getting started is often the hardest part. Jump in and it will be easier to keep going.
- Study your difficult or boring subjects first when you have the most energy.
- Learning styles matter. Know your own and use the study tips associated with it.

Step 8 – **Use Good Test-Taking Strategies**
- Arrive early, or at least on time for a test.
- Does it make more sense for you to answer all the easy questions, or move on to the hard ones first?
- Mark questions you need to return to.
- Always answer True/False and Multiple Choice questions whether you are confident of the answers or not.
- Check your answers before turning it in. Be one of the last students out the door. Take your time.

Step 9 – **Reduce Subject-Related Anxiety**
- Think back to when you started having trouble with a particular school subject. What was going on? Who was your teacher? How did you feel? See if there is an answer

SECTION I: CREATING

to why the subject makes you anxious. Sometimes knowing that is the key to overcoming the problem.

- Make sure you know all the background information necessary to understanding the class you're in. If you don't, go back and review. Ask your instructor where the gaps in your learning might be and see if they can recommend some study resources for you.

- Realize that there are many different types of thinking and learning, and you have the ability to try new methods and succeed.

Step 10 – **Use the Resources Available to You**
- Clubs and Groups on Campus
- Academic Counselors
- Career Counselors
- Computer Labs
- Financial Aid
- Library
- Counseling
- Tutors

In addition to everything else, FOCUS. Your goal while in college isn't to become the most popular person on campus, to break a record for party attendance, or to engage in as much irresponsible behavior as possible. Excessive drinking, promiscuous behavior, and drug experimentation are *not* a part of your coursework. Don't waste time, talent, or resources. Remember why you enrolled. Remember that your choices can have lifelong consequences. Your goal is to graduate, with honors if possible, and on time. Focus on your college requirements because your ultimate goal is to be the healthy, happy bearer of a well-earned degree.

SECTION I: CREATING

NOTES

C3 Creating Career Connections

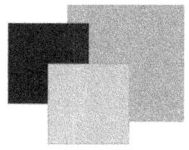

SECTION II: CAREER

CAREER

"Your work is going to fill a large part of your life, and the only way to be truly satisfied is to do what you believe is great work. And the only way to do great work is to love what you do. If you haven't found it yet, keep looking. Don't settle. As with all matters of the heart, you'll know when you find it."

-Steve Jobs

Choosing a career path can be difficult, taxing, stressful, to some even mortifying; but yet at the same time fulfilling. There are six major things you should consider when identifying a career path.

- Do I have the necessary requisite education and/or skill set to succeed?
- Do the requirements of the position line up with my personal values?
- Is this my passion?
- Will I be motivated in this line of work?

SECTION II: CAREER

- Is this something that I believe that I have been "called" to do?
- Would I do it whether I was compensated or not?

One way to answer these questions is to take career pathways assessments. Assessments can help you sort out your skills, interests, and personality to see how they fit with specific careers.

There are many assessments available, FREE, via the internet. It's important to make certain that the Assessments you chose are valid and non-biased. Most of these have associated costs due to the research necessary to develop the Assessment Tool.

Free, valid assessment tools can be found at www.dol.gov. One of the most popular and commonly used Assessment Tools is O*NET. O*NET can be accessed through the Department of Labor website.

O*NET is referred to as an interest profiler. The O*NET Interest Profiler (IP) is a self-assessment career exploration tool that can help clients discover the type of work activities and occupations that they would like and find exciting. Individuals learn from broadly presented information and identify areas of interest. They can use their interest results to explore the world of work.

The O*NET Career Exploration Tools are a set of career exploration and assessment tools that help individuals (workers and students) identify their work-related interests and abilities

C3 Creating Career Connections

and what they consider important on the job, so that they can explore occupations that match their interests, abilities, and preferences. The O*NET Interest Profiler and Computerized Interest Profiler measure six types of occupational interests (work areas):

Realistic
Investigative
Artistic
Social
Enterprising
Conventional

The Career Exploration Tools include: (1) O*NET® Interest Profiler (paper-and-pencil and computerized versions); (2) O*NET® Work Importance Locator and Work Importance Profiler (paper-and-pencil and computerized versions, respectively); and (3) O*NET® Ability Profiler. Users may download many of these materials by clicking on Career Exploration Tools at www.onetcenter.org/tools.html

SECTION II: CAREER

CDDQ.org is an anonymous site that was established to assist you in making better career decisions. The site provides access to seven free Assessments. The assessments are not time-consuming. They can be completed and feedback received in less than 15 minutes.

CDDQ-CAREER DECISION-MAKING DIFFICULTIES QUESTIONNAIRE

o   Goal: To locate the focuses of your career decision-making difficulties and to recommend ways to overcome them.
o   5 – 8 Minutes

CCDD-COPING WITH CAREER DECISION-MAKING DIFFICULTIES QUESTIONNAIRE

o   Goal: To enable you to learn about your strategies of coping with career decision-making difficulties.
o   6 – 9 Minutes

EPCD-EMOTIONAL AND PERSONALITY RELATED CAREER DECISION DIFFICULTIES

o   Goal: To provide you with feedback about the causes of your career decision-making difficulties, and recommend ways of dealing with them.
o   7 – 10 Minutes

CDMP-CAREER DECISION MAKING PROFILE (STYLE)

o   Goal: To enable you to learn about your career decision-making profile style.
o   6 – 9 Minutes

PC-PREFERENCE CRYSTALLIZATION

o   Goal: Provide feedback about the degree to which your career preferences are crystalized; that is, how well you know what you're looking for in your future career.
o   8 – 12 Minutes

SECTION II: CAREER

PIC-PRE-SCREENING, IN-DEPTH EXPLORATION, CHOICE

o   Goal: To provide you with a systematic, 3-stage process leading to making a better career decision.

o   Completion Time Varies Depending on User

CHOICE

o   Goal: To help you compare a few alternatives on your final shortlist so you can choose the best one.

o   10 – 14 Minutes

(For more information, and to take any of these Assessments visit: www.cddq.org.)

After you have completed Assessments, you should develop a list of possible jobs. When developing your list, be sure to consider whether you are willing to relocate and whether you are willing to perform shift work or weekend work. Two more areas of consideration are the job outlook and labor market. It's good to know if what interests you is a growing or decreasing career field. The U.S. Department of Labor's Bureau of Labor Statistics tracks this type of information. See www.bls.gov.

Before you can apply for any position, you'll need a resume. You should draft the resume yourself, research resume writing services, or invest in a career coach who also specializes in resume writing.

C3 CreatingCareerConnections

It's important to have more than one resume. You should consider customizing your resume to fit positions of interest. On the next page, an outline is provided that highlights what should be included in a resume.

SECTION II: CAREER

SUSIE Q. EXAMPLE

654 Sample Lane, Danville, VA 24541

555.987.1234

SQExample@gmail.com

PROFESSIONAL SUMMARY

Enter a brief description of your professional background. You can choose to highlight specific skills, knowledge or industry experience.

CORE QUALIFICATIONS

Create 2 columns and Enter 3 – 4 Skills in each.

EXPERIENCE

Enter details about your daily tasks. Start with your responsibilities, but also include results and achievements. Remember to also include any experience as a volunteer.

EDUCATION

Enter any colleges, universities, or training programs that you have completed.

PROFESSIONAL AFFILIATIONS

Enter the names of organizations in which you participate, are a member, or hold positions of leadership.

SECTION II: CAREER

To find advertised positions, visit the following job sites:

Website: Federal Government Jobs
URL: https://www.usajobs.gov/

Website: State Government Jobs
URL: http://www.jobbankinfo.org/default.aspx

Website: America's Job Exchange
URL: http://www.americasjobexchange.com/
Search for jobs on America's Job Exchange by keyword, location, or industry. Jobseekers can upload resumes, receive notifications when jobs of interest become available, access a comprehensive set of career management tools, and find resources for veterans, ethnic groups, and individuals with disabilities.

Website: Careerbuilder.com
URL: www.careerbuilder.com
CareerBuilder.com allows jobseekers to search by industry, location, company or job type; sign up for automatic email job alerts; and get advice on job hunting and career management. Also provides free job search tools such as an interactive Career Test and a Salary Calculator.

C3 Creating Career Connections

Website: EmploymentGuide.com
URL: http://www.employmentguide.com
EmploymentGuide.com provides a one-click job search for hourly and skilled jobs, from entry- to mid-management level. Jobseekers can browse by industry or keyword as well as access job search and interview tips, career advice, industry news, college programs and more.

Website: Flipdog
URL: www.flipdog.com
FlipDog lets job searchers quickly search the Monster.com database of jobs by job title, keyword, or location.

Website: US.jobs
URL: http://us.jobs/
US.jobs provides job seekers with access to job openings collected by the National Labor Exchange from more than 9,000 corporate career websites and from the state job banks. Search unduplicated, verified listings by keyword or location. Also find career resources including a salary calculator, resume help, career research, and more.

SECTION II: CAREER

Website: Jobs.com
URL: www.jobs.com
Jobseekers can browse jobs by location, category, keywords, company, or job title on Jobs.com, a member of the Monster network. Also filter results by job requirements and job types, and find career tools and advice.

Website: Monster.com
URL: www.monster.com
Job seekers can search listings by job title, keyword, industry, company or location. Also access job search, networking, resume, and career resources.

Website: Indeed
URL: http://www.indeed.com
Indeed.com is a search engine for jobs. Job seekers - Search millions of jobs from thousands of job sites, newspapers, associations and company career pages.

Recruiters also seek out employable individuals. To increase your chances of a recruiter gaining access to your resume, consider posting your resume to the sites listed above and consider creating a profile in LinkedIN. (See Section III: Connections for more information on LinkedIN).

To quickly access any or all of the above sites, visit: http://www.jobbankinfo.org/privateJobBanks.aspx#America's Job Exchange

COVER LETTERS

A cover letter complements a resume. A cover letter can cause your resume to stand out from the others and encourage a hiring official to more closely review your resume. The Harvard Business Review (http://blogs.hbr.org/2014/02/how-to-write-a-cover-letter/) in a discussion with Jodi Glickman, a communications expert and author of Great on the Job and John Lees, a UK-based career strategist and author of Knockout CV, shares these tips when writing your cover letter:

DO YOUR RESEARCH FIRST

Before you start writing, find out more about the company and the specific job you want. Look at the company's website, its executive's biographies, Twitter feeds, Facebook pages, and employee profiles on LinkedIn. Do research beyond reading the job description. Find out what challenges the company is facing, and how your role would help address or solve them. Knowing the company better also helps you decide on the right tone to use in your cover letter. Think about the culture of the organization to which you're applying. If it's a creative agency, like a design shop, you might take more risks but if it's a more conservative organization, like a bank, less may very well be more.

OPEN STRONG

People typically write themselves into the letter with "I'm applying for X job that I saw in Y place." That's a waste of text. Instead, lead with a strong opening sentence. Start with the punch line. Immediately address why this job is exciting to you and why you are the right individual for it. For example, you might write, "I am an environmental fundraising professional. I have more than 15 years of experience, and I would love to bring my expertise and enthusiasm to your growing development team." Chances are, the hiring manager or recruiter is reading a stack of letters and resumes. You want to arrest their attention, but don't mistake clever or funny for inappropriate. Humor can often fall flat or sound self-serving—even immature. Stay away from common platitudes, too. Say something direct and dynamic, such as "Before you read any further, I'd like to highlight two reasons why you might want to hire me."

If you have a personal connection with the company, or someone who works there, also mention it in the first sentence or two. Always address your letter to someone directly. With the accessibility of the internet and social media, there's no excuse to not be able to find the hiring manager's name.

EMPHASIZE YOUR PERSONAL VALUE

Hiring managers are looking for people who can help them solve problems. Drawing on the research you conduct, show that you know what the company does and some of the challenges it faces. The information doesn't need to be highly detailed, but you might mention a trend that's affected the industry. For example, you might write, "Many healthcare companies are grappling with how changing legislation will affect their ability to provide high-quality care." Then talk about how your experience has equipped you to meet those needs; perhaps explain how you solved a similar problem in the past or share a relevant accomplishment.

CONVEY ENTHUSIASM

Make it clear why you want the position. In today's economy, many people have the right skills, but employers prefer someone who really wants the job. Enthusiasm conveys personality. It may help to write something like "I'd love to work for your company! Who wouldn't? You're the industry leader, setting standards that others only follow."

SECTION II: CAREER

Don't bother applying if you're not excited about some aspect of the company or your prospective role in it. Sending out 100 résumés is time consuming and may yield no results. Identify 10 companies for which you'd love to work. Put some heart and soul into it! At the same time, don't go overboard with the flattery or say anything you don't sincerely mean. Authenticity is crucial. You don't want to sound like a gushing teenager. Be professional and mature. In some industries, like fashion or technology, it's more appropriate to say how much you love a company's product or services. A good rule of thumb is to "use only the kind of language that the hiring manager would use with one of his customers."

BE BRIEF

Much of the advice out there tells you to restrict your cover letter to a single page--even shorter is better. Most cover letters are much too long. It should be brief enough that someone can glean important information at a glance. You do have to cover a lot of ground—but you should do it succinctly.

C3 Creating Career Connections

WHEN YOU CAN'T SUBMIT A COVER LETTER

In the black hole of an online system, the rules may be different. Many companies now use online application systems that don't allow for a cover letter. You may be able to figure out how to include one in the same document as your résumé but that's not a guarantee, especially when some systems only allow for data to be entered into specific boxes. In these cases, use the format you're given to demonstrate your ability to do the job and your enthusiasm. If possible, you may try to find someone who you can send a brief follow-up email highlighting a few key points about your application.

The Harvard Business Review also lists "Principles to Remember: Do's and Don'ts".

DO:

- Have a strong opening statement that makes clear why you want the job and why you're right for it
- Be succinct — a hiring manager should be able to read it at a glance
- Share an accomplishment that shows you can address the challenges the employer faces

SECTION II: CAREER

DON'T:

- Try to be a comedian — too often that falls flat
- Send a generic cover letter — customize each one for the specific job
- Go overboard with flattery — be professional and mature

INTERVIEWS

The next step to landing a job is to ace the interview. Receiving an interview request from an employer can be both exciting and nerve racking. You may begin to ask yourself; what should I wear, how am I supposed to answer the questions, will my nerves impact my ability to perform well, will an unsuccessful interview attempt negate my chances of being selected?

Many organizations have in-house workforce development initiatives. These programs assist individuals in professional growth and development. The Washington state government posts a "WorkSource" guide on their site at www.wa.gov. The information below is from the "Interview Preparation" section of the Washington state "WorkSource" guide. For the entire guide, see: http://www.wa.gov/esd/guides/jobsearch/strategy/interview_effective.htm.

The interview is one of the most important elements in the job search process. When an employer invites you to an interview, he or she is indicating an interest in bringing you on board. The interview gives both of you the opportunity to

SECTION II: CAREER

exchange enough information to determine if you are a good "fit" for each other. Think of an interview as a highly focused professional conversation. You should use the limited amount of time you have to learn about an employer's needs and discuss the ways you can meet these needs. In many cases, you will interview at least twice before being hired for a position. Once in a brief screening interview and at least once again in a more serious meeting when you may also speak with many of your potential coworkers.

The job interview is a strategic conversation with a purpose. Your goal is to show the employer that you have the skills, background and ability to do the job and that you can successfully fit into the organization and its culture. The interview is also your opportunity to gather information about the job, the organization, and future career opportunities to figure out if the position and work environment are right for you.

Most employers do not hire people based on merit alone. Personality, confidence, enthusiasm, a positive outlook, and excellent interpersonal and communication skills count heavily in the selection process.

After your cover letter and résumé, the interview is your best opportunity to wow the employer-regardless of your background and experience. To do this, use every possible strategy to develop effective interviewing skills. The best way is to prepare a selective presentation of your background, thoughtful answers to potential interview questions, well-researched questions about the organization, and an effective strategy to market yourself. Also consider your career goals and what the available job offers, so that you can discuss both of these topics with employers. Acing an interview is a skill that improves and becomes easier with practice. Check with your school career center or your local Employment Service office to see if it offers workshops and individual videotaped mock interviews for practice.

RESEARCH

It is to your advantage to carefully research the job and the organization. There are many ways to do this. You can request printed materials from the employer, such as annual reports and job descriptions. This is an entirely appropriate request, so don't hesitate to make it. Use your library and career center resources. Ask colleagues, friends, and faculty about the organization, and about any personal contacts at the organization they might have. Look at the organization's home page. Knowing about the job will help you prepare a list of your qualifications so that you can show, point by point, why you are the best candidate.

SECTION II: CAREER

PRACTICE, PRACTICE, PRACTICE

Practice answering questions with a friend, or in front of a mirror. Ask your friend to give you constructive criticism on your speaking style, mannerisms, and poise. As you practice, avoid colloquialisms, such as "like" and "you know." Make sure you don't script all your answers-you'll sound as though you're reading cue cards! It's important to prepare yourself for talking with complete strangers.

KNOW THE LOGISTICS

The more you know, the more focused your answers will be. Find out when the interview is scheduled, where it will be conducted, what to expect as it takes place, and how long you will be there. Also find out if you will be talking to just one person, or to several.

BE PROMPT AND PROFESSIONAL

Always arrive early. If you don't know where the organization is located, call for exact directions in advance. Leave some extra time for any traffic, parking, or unpredictable events. If you are running late, call right away and let someone know. The best time to arrive is approximately 5 - 10 minutes early. Give yourself the time to read your résumé one more time, to catch your breath, and to be ready for the interview. Once you're at the office, treat everyone you encounter with respect. Be pleasant to everyone as soon as you walk in the door.

Please. Turn OFF your cell phone. Don't set it to vibrate. Don't just turn off the ringer. Turn it off! Few things are more distracting, disrespectful, disruptive and potentially damaging in a professional environment than a ringing, beeping, chiming, talking, music playing cell phone. What's worse is observing the startled interviewee scrambling to answer the call, text the caller, or find the phone before the noise stops.

DRESS FOR SUCCESS

Remember. You are not going to the beach, the gym, a park, a party, or a speed dating event. Wear a professional business suit. This point cannot be emphasized enough. First impressions are extremely important in the interview process. Women should avoid wearing too much jewelry and make up. Avoid revealing or too-tight clothing. Men should avoid flashy suits or wearing too much cologne. It is also important that you feel comfortable. While a suit is the standard interview attire in a business environment, if you're not sure if the workplace is an informal environment or not, call beforehand and ask. You can never be overdressed if you are wearing a tailored suit.

SECTION II: CAREER

BE ORGANIZED

Carry a portfolio notepad or at the very least a manila file folder labeled with the employer's name. Bring extra résumés and have the names, addresses and phone numbers of references, in case the employer asks for them. Also, bring a list of questions for the employer. You may refer to your list of questions to be sure you've gathered the information you need to make a decision. Do not be preoccupied with taking notes during the interview.

KNOW YOURSELF

You will make the interview process easier for the employer if you volunteer relevant information about yourself. Think about how you want to present your strengths, experiences, education, work style, skills, and goals. Be prepared to supplement all your answers with examples that support the statements you make. It is also a good idea to review your résumé with a critical eye and identify areas that an employer might see as limitations or want further information. Think about how you can answer difficult questions accurately and positively, while keeping each answer brief.

BE HONEST

An interview gives the employer a chance to get to know you. While you do want to market yourself to the employer, answer each question with an honest response.

BE POSITIVE

Never say anything negative about past experiences, employers, or courses and professors. Always think of something positive about an experience and talk about that. You should also be enthusiastic. If you are genuinely interested in the job, let the interviewer know that.

DISPLAY INTEREST

One of the best ways to show you are interested in a job is to demonstrate that you have researched the organization prior to the interview. You can also show interest by asking questions about the job, the organization, and its services and products. The best way to impress an employer is to ask questions that build upon your interview discussion. This shows you are interested and paying close attention to the interviewer. It is a good idea to prepare a few questions in advance, but an insightful comment based on your conversation can make an even stronger statement.

At the end of an interview, it is appropriate for you to ask when you may expect to hear from the employer.

TALK MONEY LATER

Find out as much as you can before the interview about the salary levels for the position you are seeking. Do not bring up the issue of salary during the first interview. If the interviewer asks about your salary expectations, give only a general answer, such as that your expectations seem to be within, or close to their range.

POST-INTERVIEW NOTES

After the interview, take time to write down the names (check spellings) and titles of all your interviewers, your impressions, remaining questions, and any information that may influence your decision to accept a position with the organization. If you are interviewing regularly, this will help you keep employers and circumstances clearly differentiated.

FOLLOW UP

You should write a thank you note within 48 hours after an interview, even if the interview (or the interviewer) was not

C3 CreatingCareerConnections

productive and/or you are not interested in the position. It is important to say thank you for the time the interviewer spent with you. This letter should be brief.

SECTION II: CAREER

QUESTIONS, QUESTIONS, QUESTIONS!

Monster.com advises that there can be many possible interview questions. It lists the Top 100 questions on the "career advice" section of their website. The questions are divided into seven categories:

1. Basic
2. Behavioral
3. Salary
4. Career Development
5. Getting Started
6. Personal
7. Brainteasers

C3 CreatingCareerConnections

"BASIC INTERVIEW" QUESTIONS

Tell me about yourself.

What are your strengths?

What are your weaknesses?

Why do you want this job?

Where would you like to be in your career five years from now?

What's your ideal company?

What attracted you to this company?

Why should we hire you?

What did you like least about your last job?

When were you most satisfied in your job?

What can you do for us that other candidates can't?

What were the responsibilities of your last position?

Why are you leaving your present job?

What do you know about this industry?

What do you know about our company?

Are you willing to relocate?

Do you have any questions for me?

SECTION II: CAREER

"BEHAVIORAL INTERVIEW" QUESTIONS

- What was the last project you headed up, and what was its outcome?
- Give me an example of a time that you felt you went above and beyond the call of duty at work.
- Can you describe a time when your work was criticized?
- Have you ever been on a team where someone was not pulling their own weight? How did you handle it?
- Tell me about a time when you had to give someone difficult feedback. How did you handle it?
- What is your greatest failure, and what did you learn from it?
- What irritates you about other people, and how do you deal with it?
- If I were your supervisor and asked you to do something that you disagreed with, what would you do?
- What was the most difficult period in your life, and how did you deal with it?
- Give me an example of a time you did something wrong. How did you handle it?
- What irritates you about other people, and how do you deal with it?

C3 Creating Career Connections

- Tell me about a time where you had to deal with conflict on the job.
- If you were at a business lunch and you ordered a rare steak and they brought it to you well done, what would you do?
- If you found out your company was doing something against the law, like fraud, what would you do?
- What assignment was too difficult for you, and how did you resolve the issue?
- What's the most difficult decision you've made in the last two years and how did you come to that decision?
- Describe how you would handle a situation if you were required to finish multiple tasks by the end of the day, and there was no conceivable way that you could finish them.

SECTION II: CAREER

"SALARY" QUESTIONS

- What salary are you seeking?
- What's your salary history?
- If I were to give you this salary you requested but let you write your job description for the next year, what would it say?

"CAREER DEVELOPMENT" QUESTIONS

- What are you looking for in terms of career development?
- How do you want to improve yourself in the next year?
- What kind of goals would you have in mind if you got this job?
- If I were to ask your last supervisor to provide you additional training or exposure, what would she suggest?

SECTION II: CAREER

"GETTING STARTED" QUESTIONS

- How would you go about establishing your credibility quickly with the team?

- How long will it take for you to make a significant ontribution?

- What do you see yourself doing within the first 30 days of this job?

- If selected for this position, can you describe your strategy for the first 90 days?

C3 Creating Career Connections

"MORE ABOUT YOU" QUESTIONS

- How would you describe your work style?
- What would be your ideal working environment?
- What do you look for in terms of culture -- structured or entrepreneurial?
- Give examples of ideas you've had or implemented.
- What techniques and tools do you use to keep yourself organized?
- If you had to choose one, would you consider yourself a big-picture person or a detail-oriented person?
- Tell me about your proudest achievement.
- Who was your favorite manager and why?
- What do you think of your previous boss?
- Was there a person in your career who really made a difference?
- What kind of personality do you work best with and why?
- What are you most proud of?
- What do you like to do?
- What are your lifelong dreams?
- What do you ultimately want to become?

SECTION II: CAREER

- What is your personal mission statement?
- What are three positive things your last boss would say about you?
- What negative thing would your last boss say about you?
- What three character traits would your friends use to describe you?
- What are three positive character traits you don't have?
- If you were interviewing someone for this position, what traits would you look for?
- List five words that describe your character.
- Who has impacted you most in your career and how?
- What is your greatest fear?
- What is your biggest regret and why?
- What's the most important thing you learned in school?
- Why did you choose the area of study in which you majored?
- What will you miss about your present/last job?
- What is your greatest achievement outside of work?
- What are the qualities of leader—good or bad?
- Do you think a leader should be feared or liked?
- How do you feel about taking no for an answer?

C3 Creating Career Connections

- How would you feel about working for someone who knows less than you?
- How do you think I rate as an interviewer?
- Tell me one thing about yourself you wouldn't want me to know.
- Tell me the difference between good and exceptional.
- What kind of car do you drive?
- There's no right or wrong answer, but if you could be anywhere in the world right now, where would you be?
- What's the last book you read?
- What magazines do you subscribe to?
- What's the best movie you've seen in the last year?
- What would you do if you won the lottery?
- Who are your heroes?
- What do you like to do for fun?
- What do you do in your spare time?
- What is your favorite memory from childhood?

SECTION II: CAREER

"BRAINTEASER" QUESTIONS

- How many times do a clock's hands overlap in a day?
- How would you weigh a plane without scales?
- Tell me 10 ways to use a pencil other than writing.
- Sell me this pencil.
- If you were an animal, which one would you want to be?
- Why is there fuzz on a tennis ball?
- If you could choose one superhero power, what would it be and why?
- If you could get rid of any one of the US states, which one would you get rid of and why?
- With your eyes closed, tell me step-by-step how to tie my shoes.

C3 Creating Career Connections

The Muse, an on-line organization that provides career advice and job search tools interviewed interview coach Pamela Skillings, job search expert Alison Doyle, Peggy McKee of Career Confidential, and hiring manager Mitch Fortner. Skillings, Doyle, McKee, and Fortner give suggestions on answering 30 questions that are the same, or *similarly* worded as the 100 above questions. The suggested answers are noted below; however, more in-depth information can be found at https://www.themuse.com/advice/ how-to-answer-the-31-most-common-interview-questions.

1. Can you tell me a little about yourself?
This question seems simple that many people fail to prepare for it. Don't give your complete employment (or personal) history for fear of leaving out something important, and don't sit there like a mute deer caught in headlights, either. Instead, give a pitch—one that's concise and compelling and that shows exactly why you're the right fit for the job. Start off with two or three specific accomplishments or experiences that you most want the interviewer to know about. Conclude by talking about how that prior experience has positioned you for the specific position.

2. How did you hear about the position?
It is another seemingly innocuous question, but it actually opens a door to a perfect opportunity to show your passion for, and connection to the company. For example, if you found out about

the job through a friend or professional contact, mention that individual's name, and share why you were so excited about the information. If you discovered the company through an event or article, share that. Even if you found the listing through a random job board, share what, specifically, caught your eye about the role.

3. What do you know about the company?
Any candidate can read and regurgitate the company's website "About" page. When interviewers ask this, they aren't necessarily trying to gauge whether you understand the mission—they want to know whether you care about it. Start with one line that shows you understand the company's goals, using a couple key words and phrases from the website, but then go on to make it personal. Say, "I'm personally drawn to this mission because…" or "I really believe in this approach because…" and share a personal example or two.

4. Why do you want this job?
Organizations want to hire people who are passionate about the job, so you should have a great answer about why you want the position. (If you don't, you should apply elsewhere.) First, identify a couple of key factors that make the role a great fit for you (e.g., "I love customer support because I love the constant human interaction and the satisfaction that comes from helping

someone solve a problem"), then share why you love the company (e.g., "I've always been passionate about education, and I think you guys are doing great things, so I want to be a part of it").

5. Why should we hire you?
This question seems forward, even rude and abrupt, but if you're asked it, you're in luck: There's no better setup for you to sell yourself and your skills to the hiring manager. Your job here is to craft an answer that covers three things: that you can not only do the work, you can deliver great results; that you'll really fit in with the team and culture; and that you'd be a better hire than any of the other candidates.

6. What are your greatest professional strengths?
When answering this question, interview coach Pamela Skillings recommends that a potential employee be *accurate*. Share your true strengths, not those you think the interviewer wants to hear). Be relevant. Choose your strengths that are most aligned with the position. Be specific. Instead of using the term "people skills," choose "persuasive communication" or "relationship building" instead. Follow up with an example of how you've demonstrated these strengths in a professional setting.

SECTION II: CAREER

7. What do you consider to be your weaknesses?

What your interviewer is really trying to do with this question—beyond identifying any major red flags—is to gauge your self-awareness and honesty. Saying, "I can't meet a deadline to save my life" is not an option. "I have no weaknesses. I'm perfect" isn't a smart response either. Strike a balance by thinking of something that you struggle with, but that you're working to improve. For example, maybe you've never been strong at public speaking, but you've recently volunteered to run meetings to help you be more comfortable when addressing a crowd.

8. What is your greatest professional achievement?

Nothing says "hire me" better than a track record of achieving amazing results in past jobs, so don't be shy when answering this question! A great way to do so is by using the S-T-A-R method: Set up the situation and the task that you were required to complete to provide the interviewer with background context (e.g., "In my last job as a junior analyst, it was my role to manage the invoicing process"), but spend the bulk of your time describing what you actually did (the action) and what you achieved (the result). For example, "In one month, I streamlined the process, which saved my group 10 man-hours each month and reduced errors on invoices by 25%."

9. Tell me about a challenge or conflict you've faced at work, and how you dealt with it.
In asking this question, "your interviewer wants to get a sense of how you will respond to conflict. Anyone can seem nice and pleasant in a job interview, but what will happen if you're hired and Gladys in Compliance starts getting in your face?" Again, you'll want to use the S-T-A-R method, being sure to focus on how you handled the situation professionally and efficiently, and ideally, closing with a happy ending, like how you came to a resolution or compromise.

10. Where do you see yourself in five years? If asked this question, be honest and specific about your future goals, but consider that a hiring manager wants to know the following:

a.) If you've set realistic expectations for your career;
b.) If you have ambition, and
c.) If the position aligns with your goals and growth.

Your best bet is to think realistically about where this position could take you, and answer accordingly. If the position isn't necessarily a one-way ticket to your aspirations, it's perfectly okay to say that you're not quite sure what the future holds, but that you see this experience playing an important role in helping you make that decision.

SECTION II: CAREER

11. What's your dream job?
Along similar lines, the interviewer wants to uncover whether this position is really in line with your ultimate career goals. While "an NBA star" might get you a few laughs, a better bet is to talk about your goals and ambitions—and why this job will get you closer to them.

12. With what other companies are you interviewing?
Companies ask this for a number of reasons, from investigating who is competing for your skills, to sniffing out whether you're serious about the industry. "Often the best approach is to mention that you are exploring a number of other similar options in the company's industry. It can be helpful to mention that a common characteristic of all the jobs you are applying to is the opportunity to apply some critical abilities and skills that you possess. For example, you might say 'I am applying for several positions with IT consulting firms where I can analyze client needs and translate them to development teams in order to find solutions to technology problems.'"

13. Why are you leaving your current job?
This is a toughie, but one you can be sure you'll be asked. Definitely keep things positive—you have nothing to gain by being negative about your past employers. Instead, frame

things in a way that shows that you're eager to take on new opportunities and that the role you're interviewing for is a better fit for you than your current or last position. For example, "I'd really love to be part of product development from beginning to end. I know I'd have that opportunity here."

If you were fired, keep it simple: "Unfortunately, I was let go," is a totally suitable answer.

14. Why were you fired?

If you get the admittedly *much* tougher follow-up question as to why you were let go (and the truth isn't exactly pretty), your best bet is to be honest (the job-seeking world is small, after all). But it doesn't have to be a deal-breaker. Share how you've grown and how you approach your job and life now as a result. If you can position the learning experience as an advantage for this next job, even better.

15. What are you looking for in a new position?

Hint: Ideally the *same* things that this position has to offer, so be knowledgeable of them and be specific.

16. What type of work environment do you prefer?

Hint: Ideally one that's similar to the environment of the company you're applying to. Be specific.

SECTION II: CAREER

17. What's a time you exercised leadership?

Depending on what's more important for the role, you'll want to choose an example that showcases your project management skills (i.e. spearheading a project from end to end, multitasking successfully) or one that shows your ability to confidently and effectively rally a team. And remember: The best stories include enough detail to be believable and memorable. Show how you were a leader in this situation and how it represents your overall leadership experience and potential.

18. What's a time you disagreed with a decision that was made at work?

Everyone disagrees with the boss from time to time, but in asking this question, hiring managers want to know that you can do so in a productive, professional way. "You don't want to tell the story about the time when you disagreed but your boss was being a jerk and you just gave in to keep the peace. And you don't want to tell the one where you realized you were wrong. Tell the one where your actions made a positive difference on the outcome of the situation, whether it was a work-related outcome or a more effective and productive working relationship."

19. How would your boss and co-workers describe you?

First of all, be honest. Remember, if you get the job, the hiring manager will be contacting your former bosses and co-workers!

Try to reveal strengths and traits you haven't discussed in other aspects of the interview, such as your strong work ethic or your willingness to pitch in on other projects when needed.

20. Why was there a gap in your employment?

If you were unemployed for a period of time, be direct and to the point about what you've been up to (and hopefully, that's a litany of impressive volunteer and other mind-enriching activities, like blogging or taking classes). Then, steer the conversation toward how you will do the job and contribute to the organization: "I decided to take a break at the time, but today I'm ready to contribute to this organization in the following ways."

21. Can you explain why you changed career paths?

Don't be thrown off by this question—just take a deep breath, and explain to the hiring manager why you've made the career decisions you have. More importantly, give a few examples of how your past experience is transferrable to the new role. This doesn't have to be a direct connection; in fact, it's often more impressive when a candidate can make seemingly irrelevant experience seem very relevant to the role.

22. How do you deal with pressure or stressful situations?

Choose an answer that shows that you can meet a stressful situation head-on in a productive, positive manner and let

SECTION II: CAREER

nothing stop you from accomplishing your goals. A great approach is to talk through your go-to stress-reduction tactics (making the world's greatest to-do list or stopping to take 10 deep breaths), and then share an example of a stressful situation you navigated with ease.

23. What would your first 30, 60, or 90 days look like in this role?

Start by explaining what you'd need to do to get motivated. What information would you need? What parts of the company would you need to familiarize yourself with? What other employees would you want to sit down with? Next, choose a couple of areas where you think you can make meaningful contributions right away. (e.g., "I think a great starter project would be diving into your email marketing campaigns and setting up a tracking system for them.") Sure, if you get the job, you (or your new employer) might decide there's a better starting place, but having an answer prepared will show the interviewer where you can add immediate impact—and that you're excited to get started.

24. What are your salary requirements?

The number one rule of answering this question is doing your research on what you should be paid by using sites like Payscale (www.payscale.com) and Glassdoor (www.glassdoor.com). You'll likely come up with a range, and we recommend stating the highest number in that range that applies, based on your experience, education, and skills. Then, make sure the hiring manager knows that you're flexible. You're communicating that you know your skills are valuable, but that you want the job and are willing to negotiate.

25. What are your interests outside of work?
Interviewers ask personal questions in an interview to "see if candidates will fit in with the culture [and] give them the opportunity to open up and display their personality, too. In other words, if someone asks about your hobbies outside of work, it's totally OK to open up and share what really makes you tick. Do keep it semi-professional, though: Revealing that you like to have a few beers at the local hot spot on Saturday night is fine. Telling them that Monday is usually a rough day for you because you're always nursing a hangover is not a good idea.

26. If you were an animal, which one would you want to be?
Seemingly random personality-test type questions like these come up in interviews generally because hiring managers want to see how you can think on your feet. There's no wrong answer here, but you'll immediately gain bonus points if your answer helps you share your strengths or personality or connect with the hiring manager. Pro tip: Come up with a stalling tactic to

buy yourself some thinking time, such as saying, "Now, that is a great question. I think I would have to say…"

27. How many tennis balls can you fit into a limousine? 1,000? 10,000? 100,000?

"Seriously?" you ask yourself. Nevertheless, take questions like this seriously. You just might be asked brainteaser questions, especially in quantitative jobs. But remember that the interviewer doesn't necessarily want an exact number—he wants to make sure that you understand what's being asked of you, and that you can set into motion a systematic and logical way to respond. So, just take a deep breath, and start thinking through the math.

28. Are you planning on having children?

Questions about your family status, gender ("How would you handle managing a team of all men?"), nationality ("Where were you born?"), religion, or age, are ILLEGAL—but they still get asked (and frequently). Of course, not always with ill intent—the interviewer might just be trying to make conversation—but you should definitely tie any questions about your personal life (or anything else you think might be inappropriate) back to the job at hand. For this question, think: "I'm not quite there yet. But I am very interested in the career paths at your company. Can you tell me more about that?"

29. What do you think our company could do better or differently?

This is a common one at startups. Hiring managers want to know that you not only have some background on the company, but that you're able to think critically about it and come to the table with new ideas. So, come with new ideas! What new features would you love to see? How could the company increase conversions? How could customer service be improved? You don't need to have the company's four-year strategy figured out, but do share your thoughts, and more importantly, show how your interests and expertise would lend themselves to the job.

30. Do you have any questions for us?

You probably already know that an interview isn't just a chance for a hiring manager to grill you—it's your opportunity to sniff out whether a job is the right fit for you. What do you want to know about the position, company, department, or team?

You'll cover a lot of ground in an actual interview, but have a few answers to *less* common questions ready to share. We especially like questions targeted to the interviewer ("What's your favorite part about working here?") or the company's growth ("What can you tell me about your new products or plans for growth?")

SECTION II: CAREER

SUCCESS AT WORK

You've identified a career that you wish to pursue, and drafted a resume and cover letter. You interviewed and have been selected for the position. Now that you *have* the job, how will you maintain the position and thrive in it?

I have interviewed and supervised hundreds of people during my career as a Federal leader. Below is a "Cheat Sheet" of suggestions that will help you "maintain" your position, while at the same time "thrive" in it and continue to experience professional growth and development.

MAINTAINANCE

- Be Timely
- Always Present a Professional Work Product
- Don't Be Cliquish
- Dress Appropriately
- No Visible Tattoos
- Wear Appropriate length skirts/dresses
- No unsightly tight jeans/pants
- Build Your Wardrobe

C3 Creating Career Connections

- Females: Start with dark skirts or pants, white and pastel colored blouses, accessories, i.e., scarves to add variety and dark professional pumps or flats.
- Males: Start with dark pants, white shirts, and several ties to add variety. If jackets are required in your work environment start with one or two sports coats that can go with different pants or buy two dark suits (blue and black).
- Don't Use Profanity....under any circumstance
- Don't Earn the Title of Office Gossiper or Problem Employee
- Be Respectful
- Your colleague/peer may eventually be your supervisor
- You never know who's *watching* you!
- Understand and be sensitive to cultural diversity
- Accept accountability for your successes *and* your failures
- Find a Mentor. Be a Mentor. A trusted and experienced advisor is invaluable.

SECTION II: CAREER

TO THRIVE

- Take advantage of training opportunities
- Go the extra mile. Volunteer for special projects
- Seek out advanced degree programs financed by the organization
- Make oneself marketable
- Develop a unique skill-Set
- Make oneself indispensable
- Pursue additional education or professional development (at your own expense, if necessary)
- Be dependable
- Understand legacy (and adjust if necessary)
- What message are you sending through your actions?
- Are you an ethical person?
- Are you viewed as trustworthy?
- Are you a team player?
- Are you a problem employee?
- Are you the office instigator?
- Do you always find yourself in the middle of *every* office controversy?

C3 CreatingCareerConnections

NOTES

SECTION II: CAREER

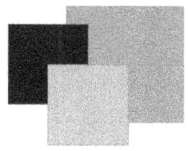

SECTION III: CONNECTIONS

CONNECTIONS

"Those who speak up-- those who use their connections are more likely to succeed than those who sit and wait."

-Madeleine M. Kunin

"It's not *what* you know, it's *who* you know." This is a common expression, and should be used as the basis for understanding the importance of networking as a strategy for career development and exploration. Effectively utilizing your connections is at the core of Networking. Whose path have you crossed?

Networking is essential to career success so much so that the United States Department of Labor collaborated with over 100 American youth to create a 147 page manual titled: Skills to Pay the Bills: Mastering Soft Skills for Workplace Success. Twenty-one of those pages are dedicated to Networking. The next several pages of this book are excerpts from the Manual. The full manual can be found at http://www.dol.gov/odep/topics/youth/softskills/softskills.pdf.

SECTION III: CONNECTIONS

Everyone has a network, even if you don't realize it, and when it comes to job searching, this network may be just as important as your skills and experience. A personal network is that group of friends, friends of friends, neighbors, teachers, bosses, and co-workers. With these people, information and experiences are exchanged for both social and potential professional reasons. Networking occurs every time you participate in a school or social event, volunteer in the community, visit with members of your religious group, talk with neighbors, strike up a conversation with someone at the store, or connect with friends online.

When networking for the purpose of career development, this means talking with friends, family members, and acquaintances about your goals, your interests, and your dreams. Most people actually learn about job openings through friends, relatives, or others who are part, of their personal network, and because each person in your network has a network of his or her own, your potential contacts can grow exponentially. This is important because more often than not, hiring managers would rather talk to a potential candidate who has been recommended by someone they either know, or currently employ.

Even if a position is not currently available, networking can lead to informational interviews that can help you not only learn about possible career paths, but also be great exposure for you to be thought of as a potential candidate when a job opens up. An information interview is not the same as a job interview by any means, but it is probably the most effective form of networking there is. In fact, according to Quintessential Careers, one out of every 12 informational interviews results in a job offer. This is a remarkable number considering the fact that research indicates that only one in every 200 resumes (some studies put the number even higher) results in a job offer.

HOW DO PEOPLE FIND JOBS?

- ➢ Talking to or contacting people you know to find job leads is the most effective way to find a job.
- ➢ Most of us find a job through personal contacts-people we already know such as our friends and family, doctor, dentist, and people we meet when we go shopping and during our normal everyday lives. Personal contacts are also the people that our friends and family know.
- ➢ Approximately 60% of job hunters find their new job with the help of friends, family members, and acquaintances.
- ➢ Other ways to find jobs include visiting career centers, employer websites, and internet job sites.

SECTION III: CONNECTIONS

PROFESSIONAL NETWORKING

Learning how to network takes time and commitment. It means seeking out people you know, people who can offer advice, as well as potential friends, and building on these relationships. Networking is finding ways to "get known' by others who can help you in your job search. It is an "active" process for developing new relationships and new opportunities. There are two major types of networking "traditional" and "social."

"Traditional" networking involves talking to people. For some networking may be an easy activity, while for others it may be scary and uncomfortable. It can also be a frightening activity. In fact, it can be so overwhelming for some that they may never attempt it! According to Lara Zielin, the author of Make Things Happen: The Key to Networking for Teens, to avoid feeling nervous or scared when networking, they should try the three P's: prepare, practice, and pull yourself together! The three P's will assist you in overcoming any fear of networking.

Google, Twitter, Facebook, YouTube, LinkedIn, Skype, and MySpace have all become synonymous with "social" networking. In fact, social media has become so popular it has its very own language! For example, you can "Google" or be "Googled." You can "friend" or "unfriend" someone on Facebook. And you can send tweets to update people on your every activity every moment of the day using your Twitter account.

C3 CreatingCareerConnections

Research shows that a large percentage of recruiters run searches of candidates on the Web to screen them; 35 percent of these same recruiters say they've eliminated a candidate based on the information they uncovered. What does this mean for young jobseekers with regard to online profiles? When using social media you should be very careful to avoid: complaining about a former employer, showing pictures of hard partying, descriptions of sexual exploits, abusive or aggressive language, etc.

Protect your online image. According to CareerBuilder.com, there are three things you can do to protect your online image – and job opportunities:

1. **Careful is the way on the information super highway. NOTHING is private.** Don't post anything on your site or your "friends" sites you wouldn't want a prospective employer to see. Derogatory comments, revealing or risqué photos, foul language, and lewd jokes all will be viewed as a reflection of your character.

2. **Exercise discretion.** If your network offers the option, consider setting your profile to 'private,' so that it is viewable only by friends of your choosing. And since you can't control what other people say on your site, you may want to use the "block comments" feature. Remember,

SECTION III: CONNECTIONS

everything on the Internet is archived, and there is no eraser!

3. **Preparation is critical.** Check your profile regularly to see what comments have been posted. Use a search engine to look for online records of yourself to see what is out there about you. If you find information you feel could be detrimental to your candidacy or career, see about getting it removed – and in the meantime make sure you have an answer ready to counter or explain "digital dirt." To practice networking activities, and to read the DOL full report on networking, visit www.dol.gov.

GETTING AHEAD: TIPS FOR SOCIAL NETWORKING

In her book "Social Networking for Career Success," Author Miriam Salpeter provides tips for using social networking to get ahead professionally. An article at www.jobs.aol.com, lists the following tips from Salpeter's book:

DON'T EXPECT SOCIAL NETWORKING TO BE A MAGIC CAREER WAND.

Job seekers must have expertise, and be willing to listen first and learn the rules of engagement. Approaching a stranger on the street to ask for a job isn't reasonable or socially acceptable, and neither is expecting strangers online to flock to help. Viable connections are the best.

DO PRESENT A CONSISTENT, PROFESSIONAL PROFILE IN SOCIAL NETWORKING BIOS.

Pick keywords people would use to identify the job or role of interest. For example, Salpeter incorporates "job search/social media coach" and "resume writer" in her profiles. Use job descriptions, company and industry websites and blogs and information from professional conference materials to identify your field's keywords. Include them in your online bios.

SECTION III: CONNECTIONS

USE ALLTOP.COM TO FIND OTHER NICHE BLOGGERS.

Regularly read and leave useful and meaningful comments on their blogs. Bloggers should generously link to and refer to colleagues in articles. Share those posts via Twitter, Facebook and LinkedIn. Be sure to include colleagues' Twitter names and/or tag them on Facebook.

USE WEFOLLOW.COM OR LISTORIOUS.COM TO FIND TWITTER USERS WHO SHARE PROFESSIONAL INTERESTS.

Search via keywords and follow selected colleagues, potential mentors, and superstars. Review their Twitter streams, retweet their posts, respond to their questions, and ask for clarification when appropriate. Don't however be a pest, create your own social networking rules and expectations, or be a stalker. Salpeter explains, "You may be surprised how a few casual tweets can result in a strong online relationship. I've even seen people build business relationships as a result of casual tweets about television shows, restaurant recommendations and sports. Don't be afraid to show your personality online!" Once there is an established connection, it's OK to ask for an introduction or advice. However, Salpeter cautions social networking users not to "jump into asking for a favor the minute the person follows you back. It's better to focus on what you can *give*."

USE ONLINE PLATFORMS TO PASS ALONG USEFUL PROFESSIONAL ADVICE AND INFORMATION.

For example, post links and insightful comments on Facebook, LinkedIn and Twitter. Remind friends, fans and followers about professional goals and skills by consistently including updates illustrating key knowledge, skills and abilities.

Informational Interviews: What They Are, and Why They Are Pertinent to Career Success

"If you want to go somewhere, it is best to find someone who has already been there."

-Robert Kiyosaki

Informational interviewing is a networking activity important to the career development and career exploration process. An informational interview is an interview with a person who is doing the kind of work in which you are interested. It is an excellent technique to use when you want to: explore different career options; learn more about certain occupations; and/ or begin to network with people who can help you in your job search. Although it is an effective job search tool, it's

C3 Creating Career Connections

very important to remember that the primary purpose of an informational interview is to obtain information, not a job.

Sample questions:

- How did you decide on this field of work?
- How did you get into this field of work?
- What do you like best about your work?
- What do you like the least?
- What is a typical day or week like for someone in your occupation?
- What kind of skills, education, and/or training would I need to get into this area?
- What personal qualities are necessary for someone in this occupation?
- What is a typical entry-level salary? (Do NOT ask how much the person you are interviewing earns!)
- Do you know someone else doing this kind of work that I could talk to for my research?

Follow up the interview with a thank you note. In it, mention the specific information that you found to be particularly interesting or helpful. Let the person know that you appreciate him/her letting you ask questions and that the information provided will be valuable to you. Also, focus on the value of the person's time and expertise. A thank you note goes a *long* way. You *want* to be remembered. ("Informational Interviews" is an excerpt from Skills to Pay Your Bills, U.S. Department of Labor, www.dol.gov.)

NETWORKING FOR BUSINESS BUILDING

If you are trying to build a business, networking is one of the most effective and least expensive marketing methods. An article at www.prosperityplace.com, by Joan Sotkin, suggests the following "10 Effective Business Networking Tips," for networking success:

1. **Choose the right venues**. Not every group of people will be right for you. Choose groups where people congregate who share your interests and/or are potential clients. Chambers of Commerce, men's and women's organizations, networking groups, special interest groups, and associations are all potential choices. Or perhaps a MeetUp.com group in your area will appeal to you.
2. **Develop relationships.** Networking is not about selling, but rather developing relationships that can lead to sales or referrals. The idea is to get to know people and allow them to get to know you. Often, people approach

networking with the hope of making a sale or getting a client after one visit to an appropriate group. That's not how it works. People do business with those they know and trust and it can take time to build up that knowledge and trust. So approach a networking event without any expectation of getting new business. Instead go with the idea of meeting new people or schmoozing with those you've already gotten to know.

3. **Dress appropriately and professionally.** Remember what is said about first impressions. Don't be a rebel. Dress in a manner that suits the workplace and your particular duties. This does not mean that you need to abandon your culture, go into debt buying expensive clothing, or be uncomfortable, but remember where you are. Leave the baggy pants and trendy costumes at home—unless you're a clown. If necessary, get advice from an image consultant. Ask someone! Don't get angry or offended if your choice of attire is addressed. Use the mirrors that are at your disposal. Can't conform? Then endeavor to be the *boss*.

4. **Prepare.** Bring plenty of business cards, but only give them to people who show a real interest in what you do. Brochures or printed postcards can also be effective. Also, craft a short description of what you do — no more than 10 or 15 seconds.

SECTION III: CONNECTIONS

5. **Ask questions** and **listen**. You don't have to talk a lot about what you do in order to find potential customers. Rather, ask people you meet questions about themselves and *their* business. Listen carefully to their answers. Find points of commonality that you can bring into the conversation.

6. **Seat yourself among people with whom you are not familiar**. Many events have walk-around networking followed by a sit-down meeting of some sort. During the walk-around, do talk to people you have met before to enhance your relationship, but sit with people you don't know in order to widen your network and meet potential customers. Here too, ask questions and listen.

7. **Talk to people who are standing alone.** People attend networking events to meet others. If someone is standing alone, that's the perfect opportunity to make a new contact. You might want to start the conversation by saying, "May I join you?"

8. **Move on – politely.** Don't spend all of your time talking to one person. Gather the information you need, exchange business cards, if appropriate, and move on. I often say, "I don't want to monopolize your time. It's been a pleasure speaking to you."

9. **Get to give.** Focus on what you can do for others, not what they can do for you. Perhaps you know someone

C3 Creating Career Connections

who could use your prospective services and vice versa. If you *do*, make the referral. Don't withhold information.

10. **Follow up.** If you make a good connection with someone, after the event, send a note saying how much you enjoyed meeting them. If appropriate, send an article or some kind of information that they might find helpful. Do not add them to your mailing list without their permission.

Sotkin concludes that networking is "a process", not a one-off event. She instructs networkers to:

1. Take the time to develop relationships with people of interest.
2. Be proactive and invite someone to a one-to-one meeting to get to know them.
3. Remember that most business owners and practitioners *are* looking for connections.

Sotkin admonishes networkers to be bold and step forward into the world of their area of expertise.

SECTION III: CONNECTIONS

NETWORKING FOR INTROVERTS

Are You An Introvert? If so, you may find networking to be exceptionally difficult, intimidating, scary, useless and overwhelming. Fight the inclination to avoid it. Networking is one of the best ways not only to share information, but to get the information you need and form valuable relationships.

According to the Myers-Briggs (Personality) Type Indicator (www.MeyersBriggs.org), Introverts are likely to:

- Be seen as "reflective" or "reserved."
- Feel comfortable being alone and like things they can do on their own.
- Prefer to know just a *few* people well.
- Sometimes spend too much time reflecting and don't move into action quickly enough.
- Sometimes forget to check with the outside world to see if their ideas really fit the experience.

C3 Creating Career Connections

In a US News, on-line article (http://money.usnews.com) Social Media Consultant, career coach, author, speaker, and resume writer Miriam Salpeter lists 10 Simple Tips to Networking Success:

1. **Become a sleuth.** Before attending in-person events, find out who *else* plans to attend. This is easier than ever--especially if you received an online invitation. Heading to a backyard barbecue? There's bound to be an e-invitation listing the guests and their RSVPs. Attending a professional event? Organizers likely used a social application to record responses and make them available to invitees. Many event organizers post their plans via LinkedIn's "Events" application. (Access it through LinkedIn's "More" tab, then navigate to "Applications" to add it to your profile.) Colleagues and potential mentors may have listed themselves as attending, which provides easy access to click through their profiles to learn about their backgrounds and interests.

2. **Research several targets**. It's not stalking; many people make a habit of googling people they expect to meet *prior to* an in-person encounter. It's commonplace to review LinkedIn profiles, Twitter streams, and even Facebook pages owned by potential networking contacts. Focus first on professional information: Learn where people

attended school, where they worked, and spend time reviewing their professional bios, or LinkedIn summaries. Make sure you have a complete LinkedIn profile in case anyone is researching *you*. Look for some common, personal touch points. Are there any connections? Do the people you will meet belong to public, online group-focused hobbies you enjoy? Make a note of any potential talking points.

3. **Search for recent press releases, broadcast or printed news reports; articles.** Have their organizations been in the news? What about the contacts themselves? Have they recently been quoted in a professional journal or online newsletter? Most people are flattered when new colleagues mention a quote or comment of theirs that received positive press. Doing so also makes it clear that a job-seeker is on top of industry news. That's always helpful.

4. **Make a list of several conversation starters.** If it's uncomfortable meeting new people, advance research and planning will come in very handy moments after a great contact extends a handshake. Maybe the person enjoys skydiving and you do too! Work the topic into the conversation. It's not necessary to say, "In researching your background, I noticed you enjoy free falling from airplanes, and so do I." Even in an age when it's easy

to find out anything about other people, this might seem a bit aggressive and weird. Instead, once niceties are exchanged, feel free to comment, "Wow! Isn't this weather is great for skydiving? I hope it lasts until the weekend." The new contact will likely pick up the topic and a *natural* conversation will ensue.

5. **Practice.** There's a reason "practice makes perfect." If conversing with strangers makes you uncomfortable, spend some time role-playing with friends or in front of a mirror. Make a list of things to say. It helps to prepare to discuss topics with buzz. See the latest movies, read some in-demand books, and watch or read the news before the event.

6. **Don't immediately ask for help.** The ability and willingness to *find* information is just as important as knowing which questions to ask. It may seem counter-intuitive, but avoid asking for help when meeting people for the first time. Do not wear a metaphorical "J" for Job-seeker on your chest by rattling off your job-search experience/history and sparkling qualifications. Make a point to have an engaging, upbeat conversation about *non*-work related topics, too. It can lead to a more formal follow-up meeting. An individual who is looking for a "hook up" can be spotted a mile away. Yes. You need employment, but don't project neediness.

SECTION III: CONNECTIONS

7. **Be a good listener.** Ask a plenty of questions. Most people enjoy talking about themselves. Be the person who wants to know *more* about new contacts. Nod, smile, make eye contact, and do everything possible to leave a favorable impression. A good conversation where the other person feels valued and heard is likely to lead to another meeting.

8. **Request a meeting.** It's so much easier to have a professional conversation in a quiet, one-on-one setting where people are not hovering around, waiting to talk to your contact. After a great introduction and casual conversation, ask for another meeting and arrange an informational interview. If the interaction is lively and pleasant, most people will *at least* agree to engage you again.

9. **Seek the best ways to reconnect.** Some people monitor Twitter or LinkedIn religiously. Others prefer voice mail or emails. Ask about the best time to reach your new friends and contacts. Avoid frustration: Use their *preferred* methods, even if it means stepping out of your comfort zone.

10. **Follow up.** It's a shame to research and plan to meet new people, have engaging conversations, and end them without obtaining contact information, or arranging subsequent meetings. Don't waste opportunities to make

C3 CreatingCareerConnections

the most of in-person meetings. If the contact agreed to meet at a later date, make a point to immediately lock in a meeting time.

SECTION III: CONNECTIONS

NETWORKING FOR EXTROVERTS

Extroverts are more likely to enjoy networking and not feel anxious when attending networking events.

Myers-Briggs (www.Myers-Briggs.org) indicates that the following statements generally apply to extroverts:

- Seen as "outgoing" or as a "people person."
- Feel comfortable in groups and like working in them.
- Have a wide range of friends, and know lots of people.
- Sometimes jump too quickly into an activity and don't allow enough time to think it over.
- Before starting a project, sometimes forgets to stop and get clarity about what they want to do and why.

Although extroverts may feel comfortable networking, there is always room for improvement. You can *always* hone your networking skills.

Http://www.Reed.eduprovides10StepstoBetterNetworking:

Step 1: **Have the right mindset.** Networking is more like farming than hunting. You will be more successful in the long run by cultivating relationships with people than by trying to close the deal in a first meeting.

Step 2: **Have networking tools with you at all times.** These include an informative name badge, business cards, a brochure, or resume. The point is to have them available *if* the conversation turns to the need for them. Handing them out indiscriminately cheapens them.

Step 3: **Act like a host, not a guest**. A host is expected to do things for others, while a guest sits back and relaxes. Make people feel welcome and comfortable. Introduce others to people you have already met, especially if they have something in common. Meet people who are standing by themselves. If you are in a group, open up to others and make it easy for them to join your circle.

Step 4: **Listen and ask questions.** Remember that a good networker has two ears and one mouth and uses them proportionately. Find out about their business as well as their outside interests.

Step 5: **Give leads or referrals whenever possible.** The best networkers believe in the givers gain philosophy. If you don't genuinely attempt to help the people you meet, then you are not networking effectively. Reciprocity builds the relationship. Success in business is the result of service and relationships.

SECTION III: CONNECTIONS

Step 6: **Small courtesies count a lot in today's world.** A thank-you note or follow-up call after someone has given you a referral shows that you value the relationship and appreciate their efforts. They are more likely to remember you and be interested in helping you again. If you see an article that might be of interest to someone, send or e-mail a copy.

Step 7: **Make a point to meet new people.** While it is more comfortable for most of us to hang out with friends and associates, your purpose at particular is functions to meet *new* people. Get out of your comfort zone. Some networking gurus suggest that you set a goal for how many people you meet or set time limits for how much time you spend with each person. I find these suggestions to be too mechanical. A professional connection with *one* person can be far more valuable than engaging 20 people who can't remember your name, don't share your interests, and can't or won't assist, mentor, or motivate you in any way. Circulate so you know who is in the room.

Step 8: **Write notes on the reverse side of the business cards you collect.** Record anything you think may be useful in remembering people or the conversations you had, especially anything you promised to do. If it is awkward to do this at the meeting, stop on your way home or in your car and write down as much as you can remember.

Step 9: **Be yourself. Be authentic.** Remember, you are building relationships that may last a long time. People trust you more when they see a consistent pattern of behavior. And trust and knowledge are the basis of developing a relationship. That said, sometimes it is just better to skip an event if you are feeling under the weather or have just gone through a major break-up in your life. You do want to present yourself in a positive and professional manner.

Step 10: **Follow up!** This is the most important part of networking. Ask for permission to call or e-mail or send information. Then do whatever you say you are going to do. If someone has helped you get an interview or gave you a referral, keep in touch and let them know how things went.

SECTION III: CONNECTIONS

You now have a tool kit full of resources you can actually *use*! You know what you need to do, and when you need to do it to better your chances of getting into college. You now have tools that teach you how to *succeed* as you pursue higher education. You are now familiar with numerous on-line job sites. You know what to wear to an interview, and how to succinctly and effectively answer questions *during* the interview. You also know the importance of coming to the interview equipped with questions of your own. In your tool kit are steps to networking, which is integral to career success. Don't let being an introvert stop you from making valuable connections with other professionals. Use the tips you now have to network effectively!

A cute, fancy, shiny tool kit will only occupy space and collect dust if you don't *open* it. Tools are meant to be *used* and there is a *proper* tool for every endeavor. *Use* your tools!!! Never stop creating ways to reach your full potential. Never stop advancing in your career and make it your priority to reach the pinnacle. Make professional connections. Continue to network. Personal and professional growth and development are rewarding. Lastly, pay it forward! The mark of a good leader is to groom someone else to take his or her place. Don't be an information hoarder! Share it!

"All Connections Matter. Change Your Circumstances by Changing Your Connections."

-Dr. Lesia M. Banks

C3 CreatingCareerConnections

NOTES

SECTION III: CONNECTIONS

REFERENCES

www.drlesiabanks.org

http://www.americasjobexchange.com

http://blogs.hbr.org/2014/02/how-to-write-a-cover-letter

http://www.careerbuilder.com

http://www.ccsf.edu

http://www.cddq.org

http://www.centerforpubliceducation.org.referenced Carnevale, A.P., Smith, N. and Strohl, J. (2010). Help Wanted: Projections of jobs and education requirements through 2018. Georgetown University Center on Education and Workforce, http://cew.georgetown.edu/jobs2018/

http://www.dol.gov/odep/topics/youth/softskills/softskills.pdf

http://www.ed.gov

http://www.employmentguide.com

http://www.firstgenerationstudent.com/blog/10-steps-freshmen-need-to-know-to-be-successful-in-college

http://www.flipdog.com

http://www.indeed.com

http://www.jobabnkinfo.org/default.aspx

http://www.jobs.aol.com

http://www.money.usnews.com

http://www.monster.com

http://www.myers-briggs.org

https:/mynextmove.dol.gov

http://www.prosperityplace.com

http://www.reed.edu

https://studentaid.ed.gov/sites/default/files/college-prep=checklist.pdf

https://www.themuse.com/advice/how-to-answer-the-31-most-common-interview-questions

http://www.usajobs.opm.gov

http://us.jobs/

http://www.usjobs.com

http://www.wa.gov/esd/guides/jobsearch/strategy/interview_effective.htm

ABOUT THE AUTHOR

Dr. Banks is the Founder and CEO of Dr. Lesia M. Banks Enterprises, LLC, a career coaching and organizational leadership consulting practice and is a certified Global Career Development Facilitator. With regard to coaching she focuses on three areas: career coaching, doctoral dissertation coaching, and small business development coaching. She is a thought partner and consultant in organizational leadership theories and practical implementation. Dr. Banks has more than 27 years of Federal government experience to include serving in various leadership positions in numerous executive branch departments. Her responsibilities have encompassed the entire spectrum of Human Capital management to include conducting hundreds of job interviews, hiring and training employees, supervising diverse staffs, and managing multi-million dollar budgets.

Dr. Banks serves as a Technical Coach for President Obama's Youth CareerConnect federal grant initiative. Her role as coach affords her the opportunity to provide technical assistance to school systems in six core program areas: Integrated Academic and Career-Focused Learning, Employer Engagement, Individualized Career and Academic Counseling, and Work-Based Learning and Exposure to the World of Work. In this role, she is assigned to the largest public school system in the entire United States; the New York City public school system, which hosts over 1.1 Million students, in more than 1,700 schools with a budget of nearly 25 Billion. Other schools under her purview also include public schools in Massachusetts, Ohio, and Buffalo, New York. Dr. Banks is also a consultant to Prometrics; an international organization tasked with developing course exams for universities and colleges around the world.

In 2014, Dr. Banks authored her first book: C^3 CreatingCareerConnections (A Pre-College to Career Enrichment Guide). First Edition.

Dr. Banks holds an Associate Degree of Applied Science in Police Science, a Bachelor of Science Degree in Sociology/Law Enforcement with a minor in Psychology, a Master's in Business Administration with a concentration in Human Resource Management and a Doctorate of Education in Organizational Leadership with a concentration in Conflict Resolution. Dr. Banks is also a 2012 Harvard University Fellow.

DR. LESIA M. BANKS
ENTERPRISES, LLC
CreatingCareerConnections℠

Coach. Author. Consultant.

www.drlesiabanks.org

☎ 260-C3BOOK3
✉ info@drlesiabanks.org
📷 @lesiabanks
🐦 @careerconnector
f @lesia.banks.3
in @drlesiambanks

www.ingramcontent.com/pod-product-compliance
Lightning Source LLC
Chambersburg PA
CBHW070554160426
43199CB00014B/2498